THIS BOOK BELONGS TO

_____

PROUD HOST SIBLING OF

_____

THERE'S SOMEONE NEW IN MY FAMILY

WRITTEN BY CARLA REY & MARCELA LAPERTOSA
ILLUSTRATED BY EUGENIA KUSEVITZKY

Copyright © 2021 by Carla Rey Vasquez & Marcela Lapertosa
All rights reserved. No part of this publication may be reproduced, stored in any form of retrieval system or transmitted in any form or by any means without prior permission in writing from the publishers except for the use of brief quotations in a book review.

Illustrated by Eugenia Kusevitzky

This is the story of Camila and her host sister Anita.
Camila will tell us about all her adventures with Anita,
but you can write your own story too!
You can ask your parents or your host siblings to help you.

My mum told us we will have someone new in our family very soon!
She will live with us for a long time and will go to school.
She will learn our language and how we do things around here.
We are hosting a student from a different country.

We got some forms with her photo on it and a letter to us.
This was my first letter ever! So exciting!
She is from a far away country, her name is Anita and she says she likes watching movies with her friends. She also enjoys gymnastics. She is very excited to meet us, and so are we!

Draw a picture of your host sibling

TELL US ABOUT YOUR NEW SIBLING

MY NEW SIBLING IS CALLED

_____

THEY SPEAK

_____

THEY COME FROM

_____

WHERE IS THAT IN THE WORLD?

We are setting up her bedroom and can't wait for her to arrive!
I always wanted a big sister.
I am so excited that I told all my friends about it.
Now they all want a big sister too.

WHEN YOUR HOST SIBLING IS HERE

WHAT WOULD YOU LIKE TO TEACH THEM?

_____

_____

WHAT WOULD YOU LIKE TO LEARN FROM THEM?

_____

_____

WHAT IS SOMETHING FUN THAT YOU WOULD LIKE TO DO WITH THEM?

_____

_____

We finally went to the airport to pick her up.
We brought some big signs with us.
She arrived with a lot of other students traveling abroad, like her.
She was very tired the first days. She is still learning English.

WELCOME TO YOUR NEW SIBLING

Make a sign for them, you can take it to the airport or put it in their room!

Anita speaks another language. I wish I could understand what she is saying. She is teaching me some words (in exchange for all the words I am teaching her) I love teaching her English!

_____ DICTIONARY

Sibling language

Ask your host sibling to write some words here and help you learn them

_____

_____

_____

_____

_____

_____

_____

_____

Anita has started school and is making new friends.
She loves fish and chips.
She also joined the local gymnastics club.

DISCOVERIES

MY HOST SIBLING REALLY LIKES

_____

_____

MY HOST SIBLING REALLY DOESN'T LIKE

_____

_____

Yesterday, she made us dinner. It was very spicy for us, but she had no issues getting through it. She is a great cook but puts spicy sauce on all meals. Maybe she can learn to make meals milder for us, and we can learn to eat a bit spicier.

_____ RECIPES
Sibling country

WHAT'S YOUR SIBLING FAVOURITE FOOD(S) FROM HERE?

Hosting Anita is great. But I have to be honest, sometimes it is a bit tricky.
For example, she says that she likes the food my parents cook, but then she does not eat it.
My parents get worried about it, but when they ask her if she is hungry she just says it is all good.

LEARNING TO LIVE TOGETHER

WHAT ARE THE MAIN CHALLENGES ABOUT LIVING WITH A HOST SIBLING?

_____

_____

_____

WHAT HAS SURPRISED YOU SO FAR?

_____

_____

_____

Anita is really happy when we play together and laughs a lot. But sometimes, when she talks to her family, she gets sad. I understand, because I also get sad when I am at grandma's and I miss my parents. So, I give her lollies or invite her to watch a cartoon with me.

LEARNING FROM DIFFERENCES

IS THERE ANYTHING THAT YOU FIND HARD TO UNDERSTAND ABOUT YOUR HOST SIBLING?

_____
_____
_____
_____
_____
_____
_____
_____

Anita is my best friend. But sometimes she tells my mum that it is hard to make real friends at school.
I do share my friends with her.
I wish people her age were more welcoming, because she deserves 1000 friends.

BEING KIND AND WELCOMING

WHAT IS SOMETHING THAT YOU OR YOUR FAMILY HAVE DONE TO MAKE YOUR HOST SIBLING FEEL WELCOMED?

The great news is that, now that she has been with us for a long time, she speaks English like a pro and everyone knows her in our neighbourhood. She has lots of friends and even has vegemite on toast for breakfast!

It is so funny because our neighbours are all wondering, "who is this someone new in our house?".

DISCOVERIES

HOW CAN YOU INTRODUCE YOUR HOST SIBLING TO OTHER PEOPLE?

The bad news is that she is going back home soon. But the best thing is that we got to have someone new in my family! And now I will have a big sister forever.

DISCOVERIES

Draw your happiest memory with your host sibling

I learned so much with Anita! I learned we are all different but we are also very similar. We might eat different food, wear different clothes and speak different languages but we all care about our families and we all need to have friends.
And I also learned that to create a better world for everyone we need to be kind, open and welcoming to those different from us.
Thank you Anita!

_____ MEMOIR

Sibling name

YOUR HAPPIEST MEMORY WITH THEM IS

_____

_____

SOMETHING YOU LEARNED FROM THEM

_____

SOMETHING YOU TAUGHT THEM

_____

MAIN CHALLENGE WAS

_____

BUT I LEARNED

_____

PHOTO ALBUM

31

WELCOM

www.ingramcontent.com/pod-product-compliance
Lightning Source LLC
Chambersburg PA
CBHW041430010526
44107CB00045B/1560